WELCOME

Please leave a review because we would love to hear your feedbacks, opinions and advice to create better products for you! Also, we would love to know how you use your **coloring book**

Thank you for your support.
You are greatly appreciated.

Find Out The Color Of This Flag

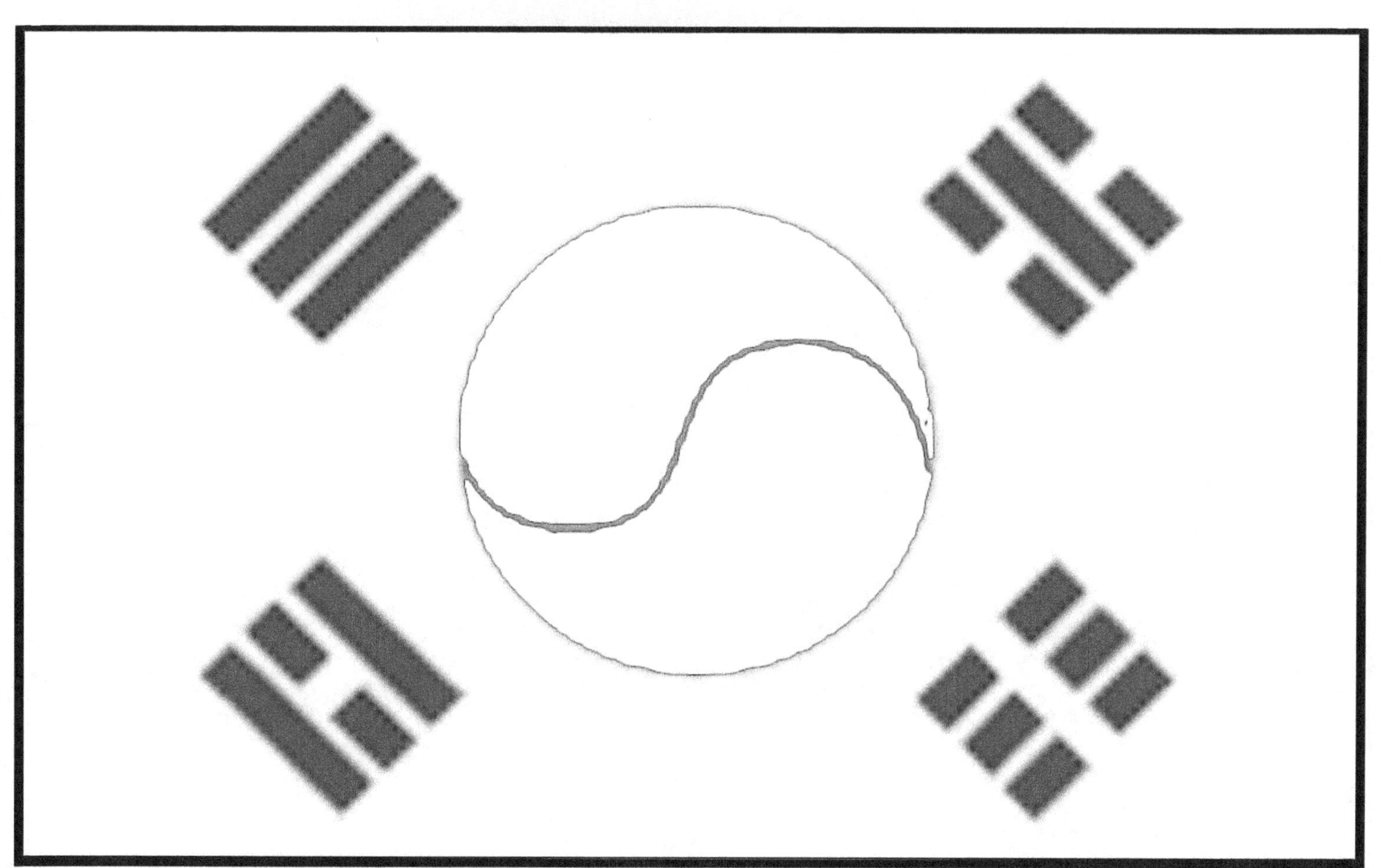

SOUTH KOREA

HONDURAS

ICELAND

ARAB EMARATES

LIBYA

NETHERLANDS

VIETNAM

RUSIA

YEMEN

Find Out The Color Of This Flag

BOLIVIA

Find Out The Color Of This Flag

ARMENIA

GABON

Find Out The Color Of This Flag

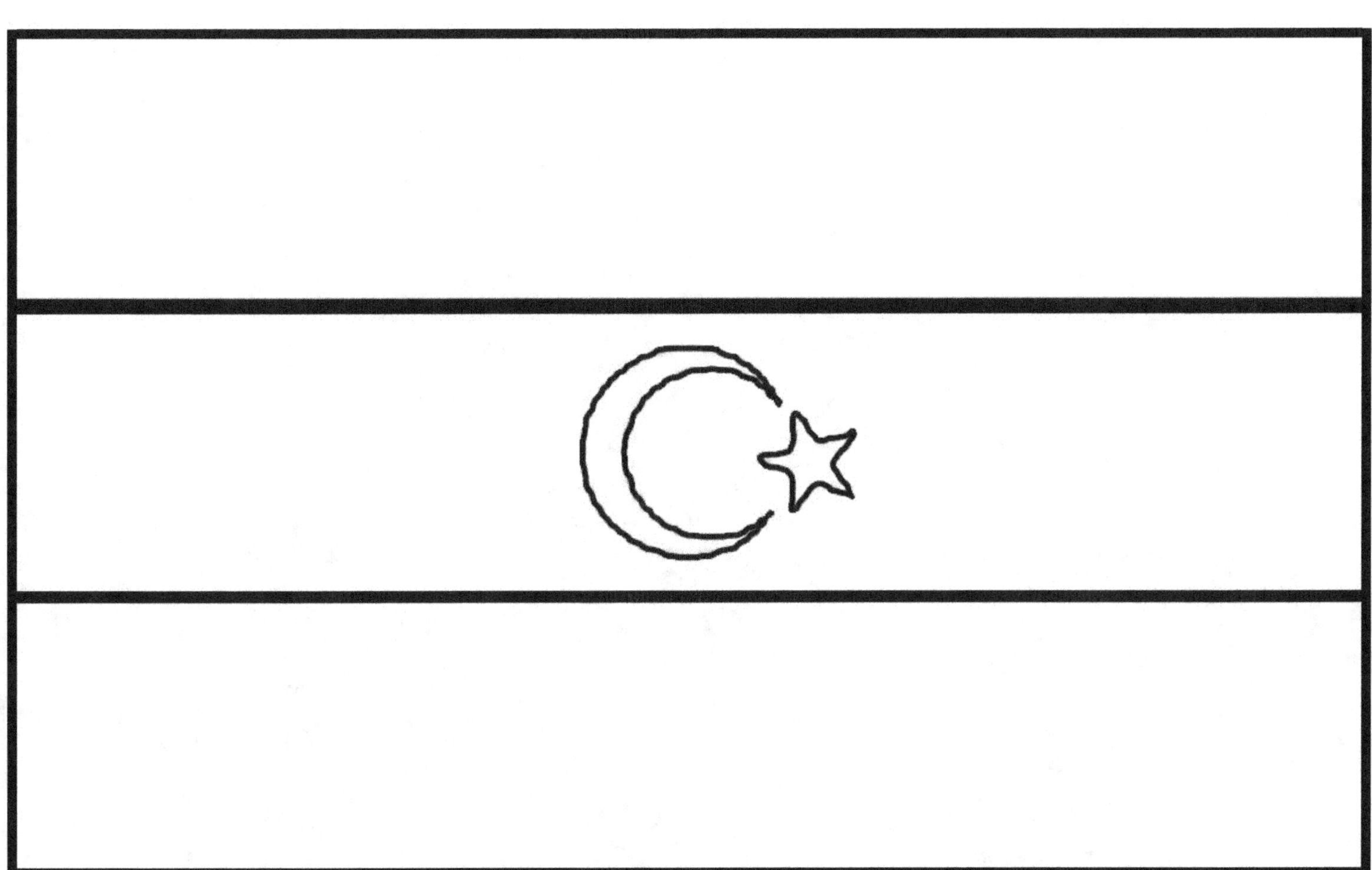

LIBYA

NIGER

ARGENTINA

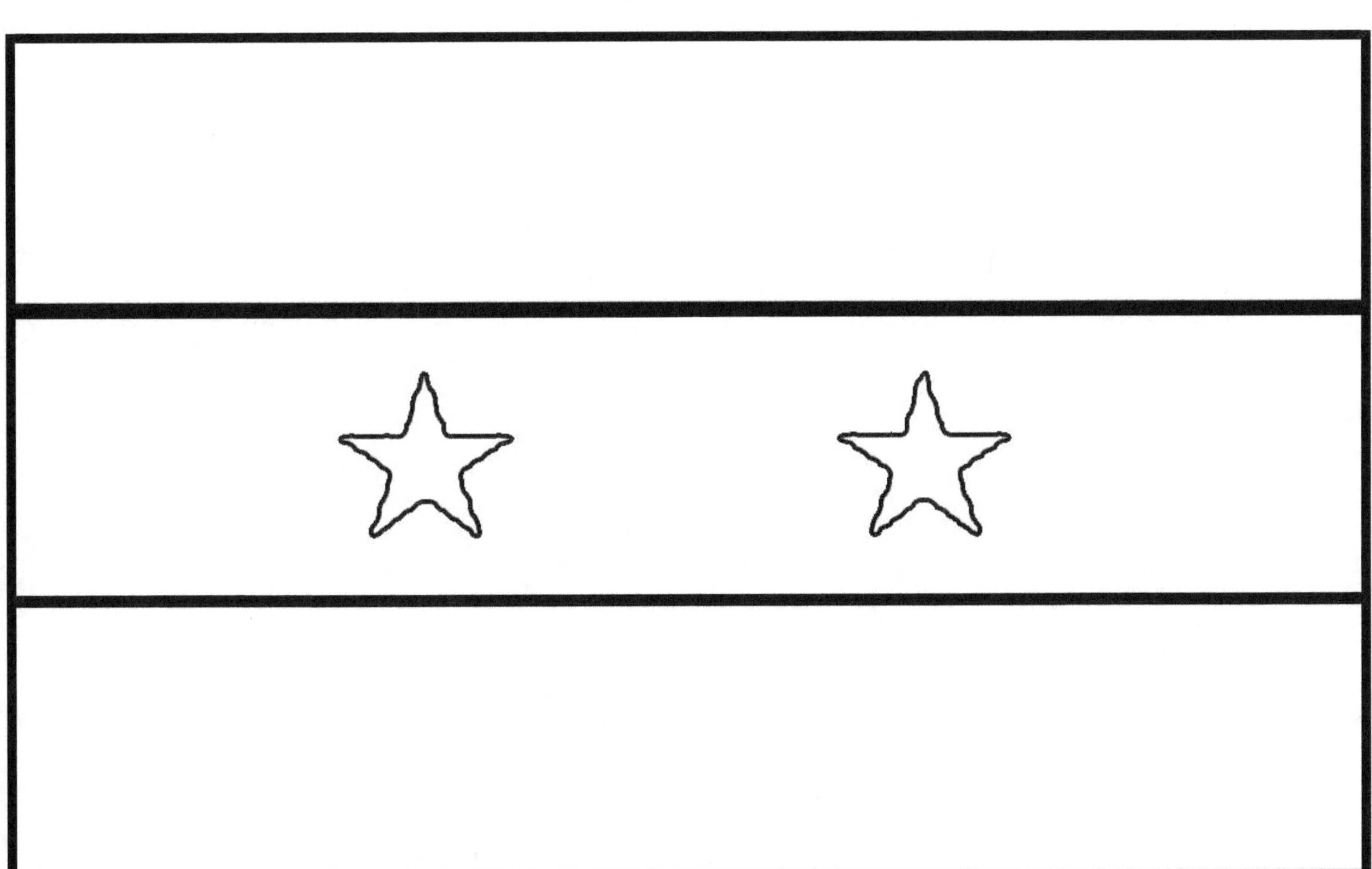

SYRIA

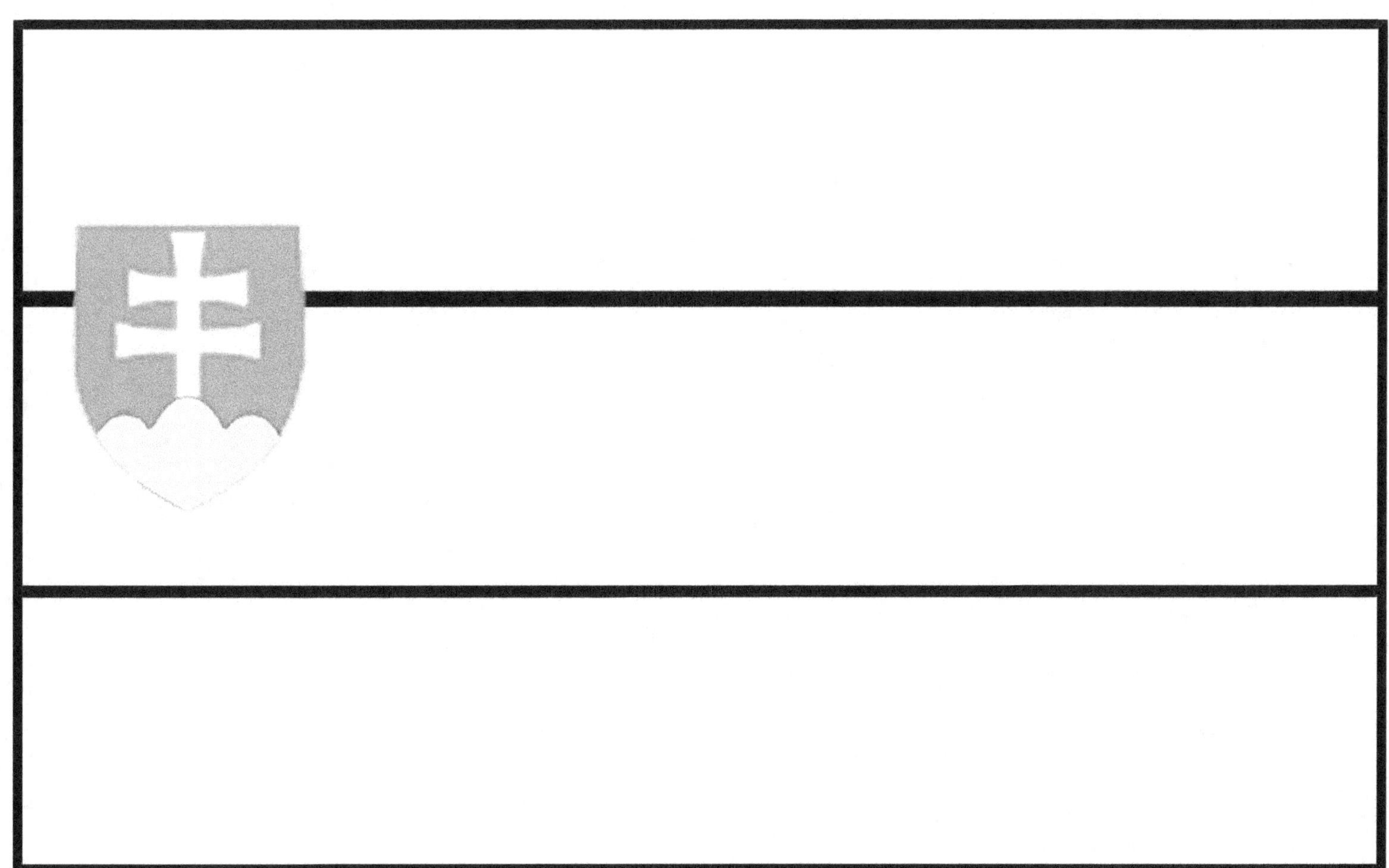

SLOVAKIA

PARAGUAY

Find Out The Color Of This Flag

REPUBLICA DE NICARAGUA
AMERICA CENTRAL

NICARAGUA

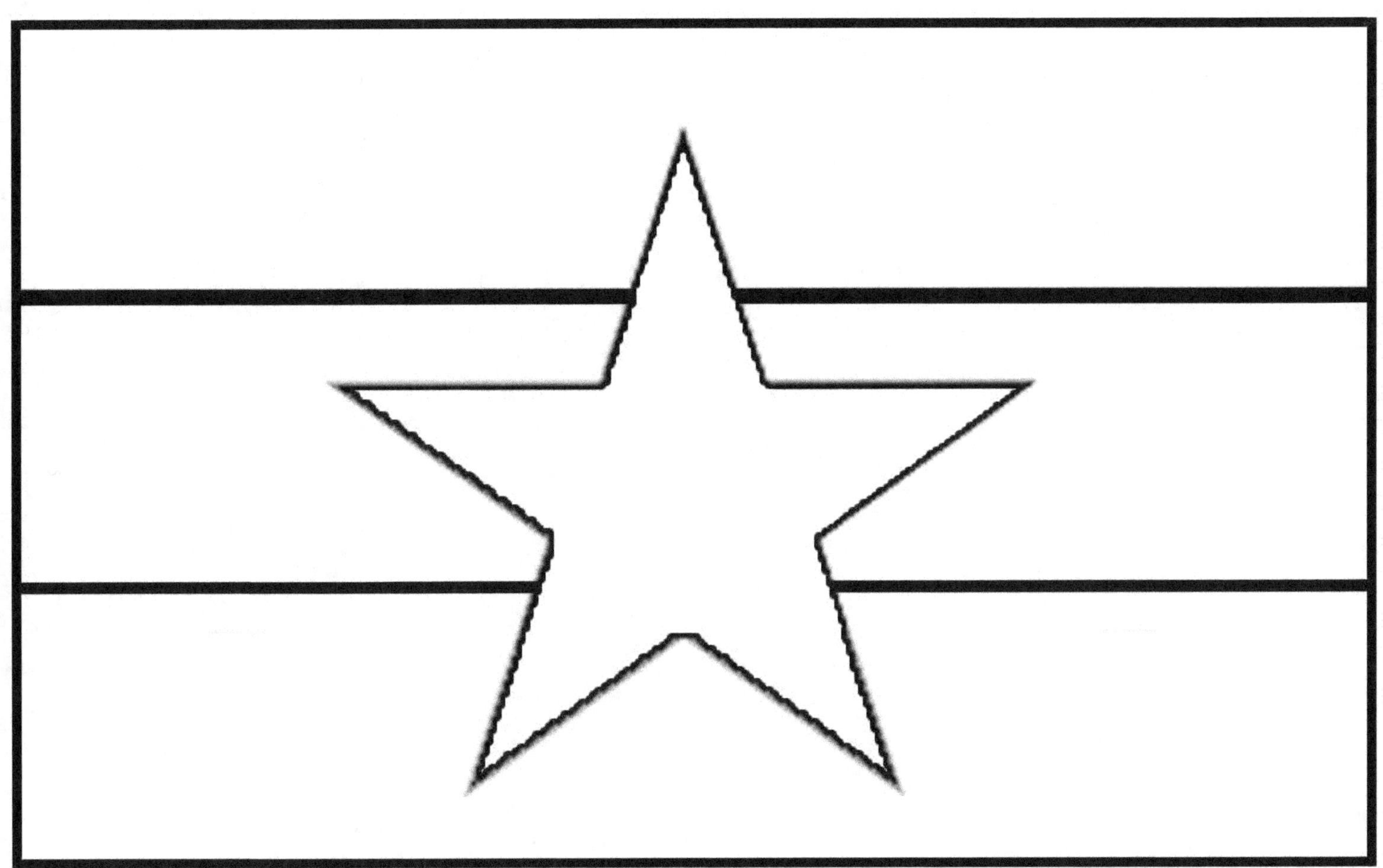

NYANMAR

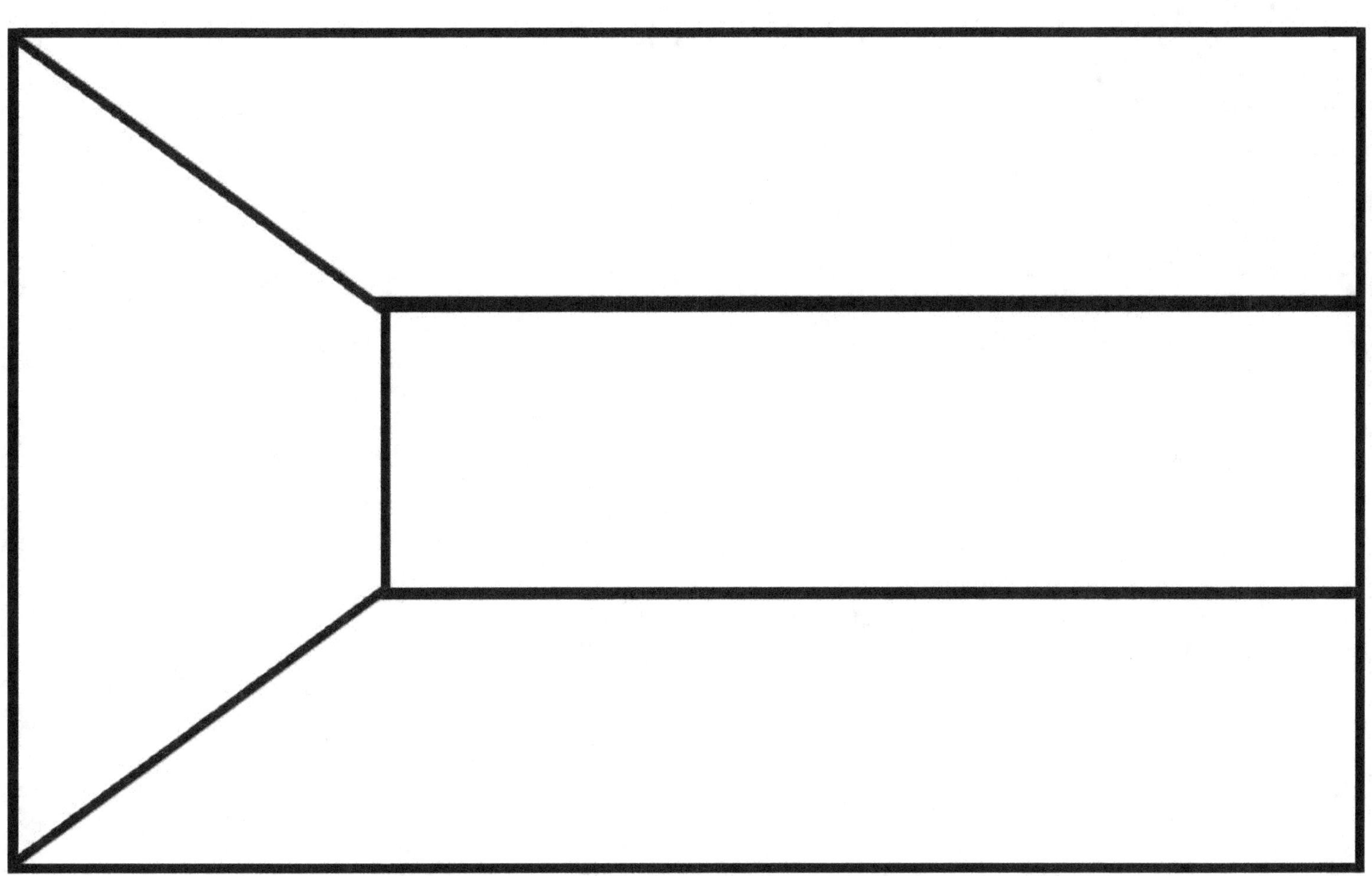

KUWAIT

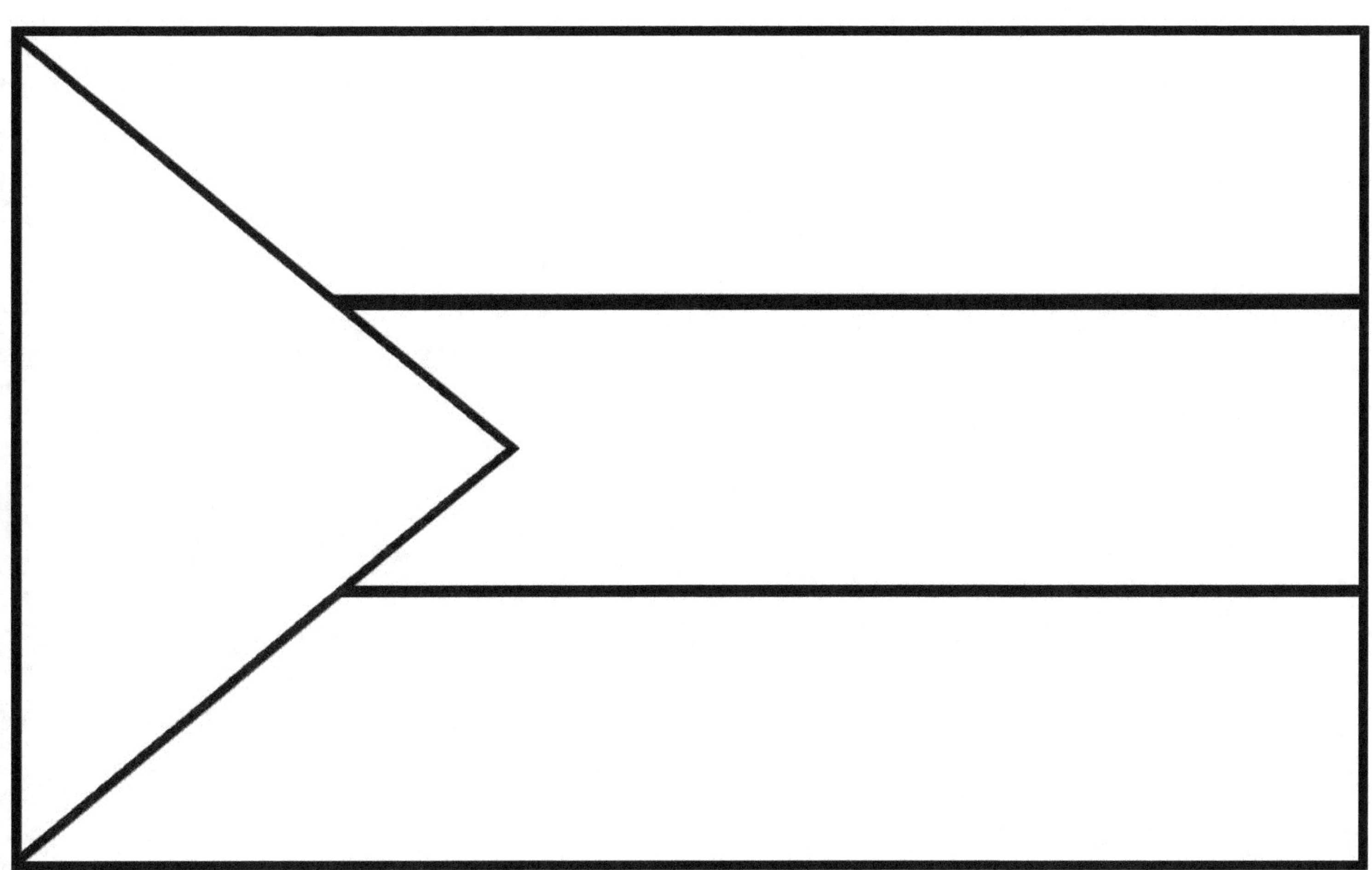

SUDAN

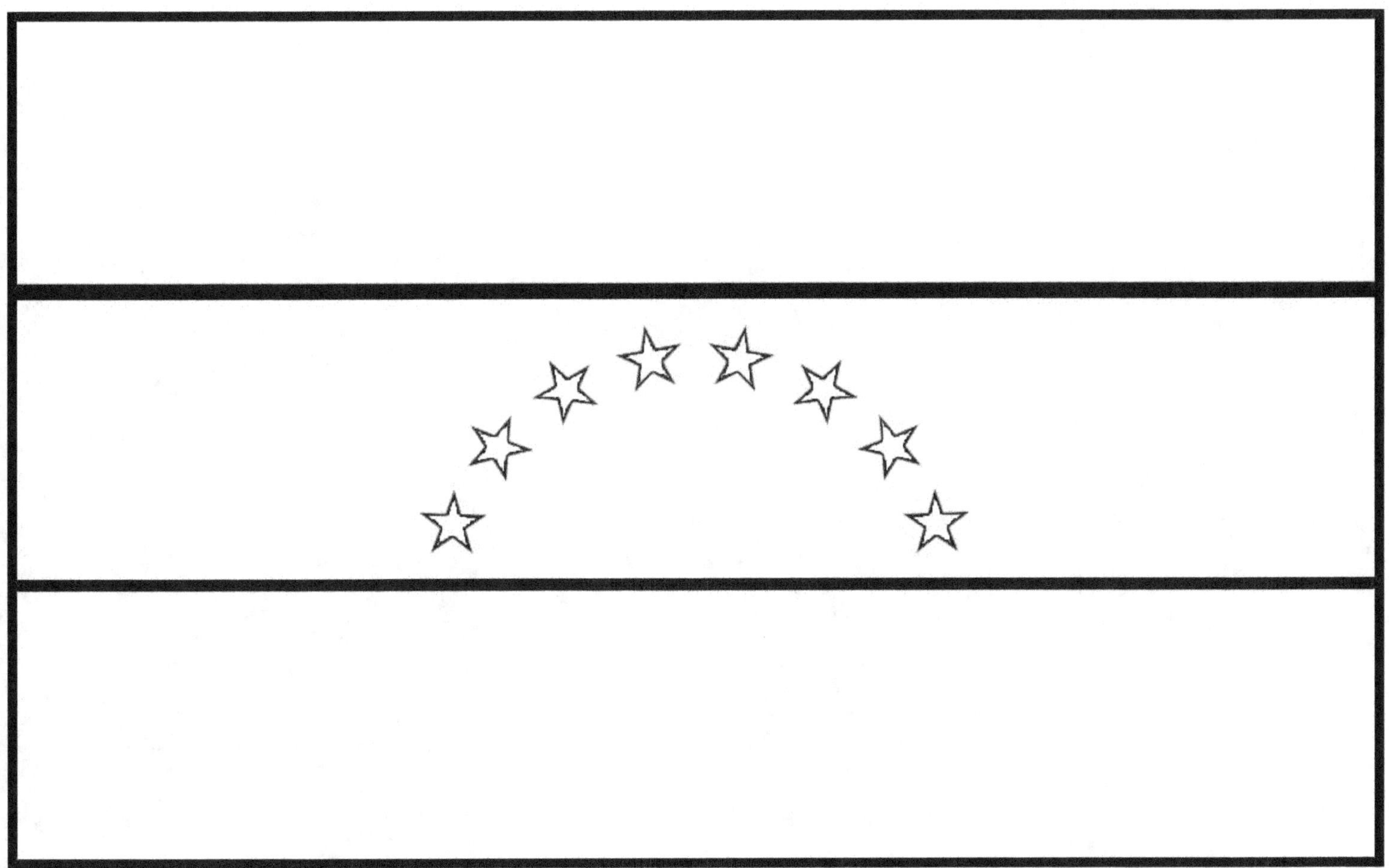

VENEZUELA

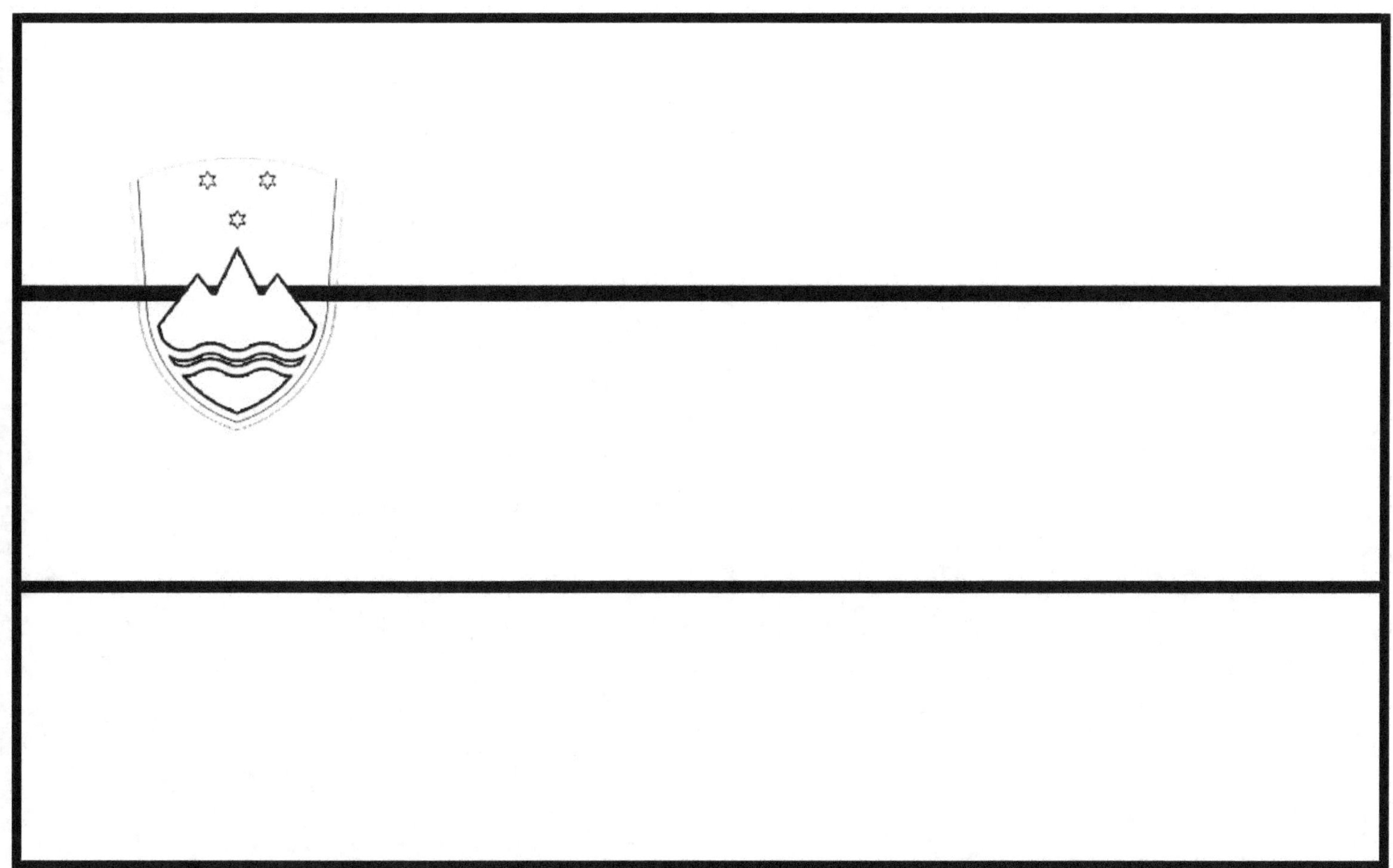

SLOVENIA

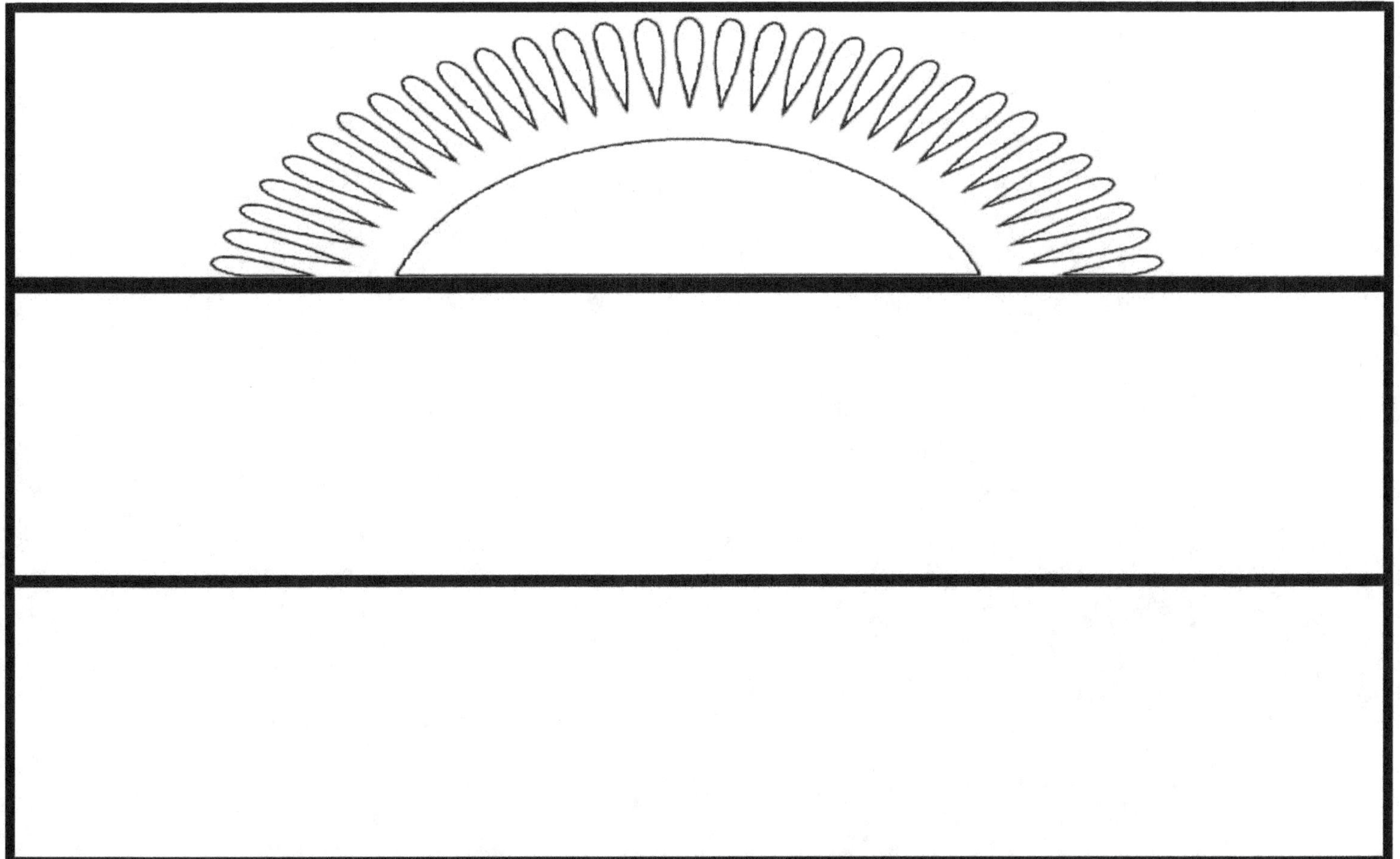

MALAWI

GERMANY

LESOTHO

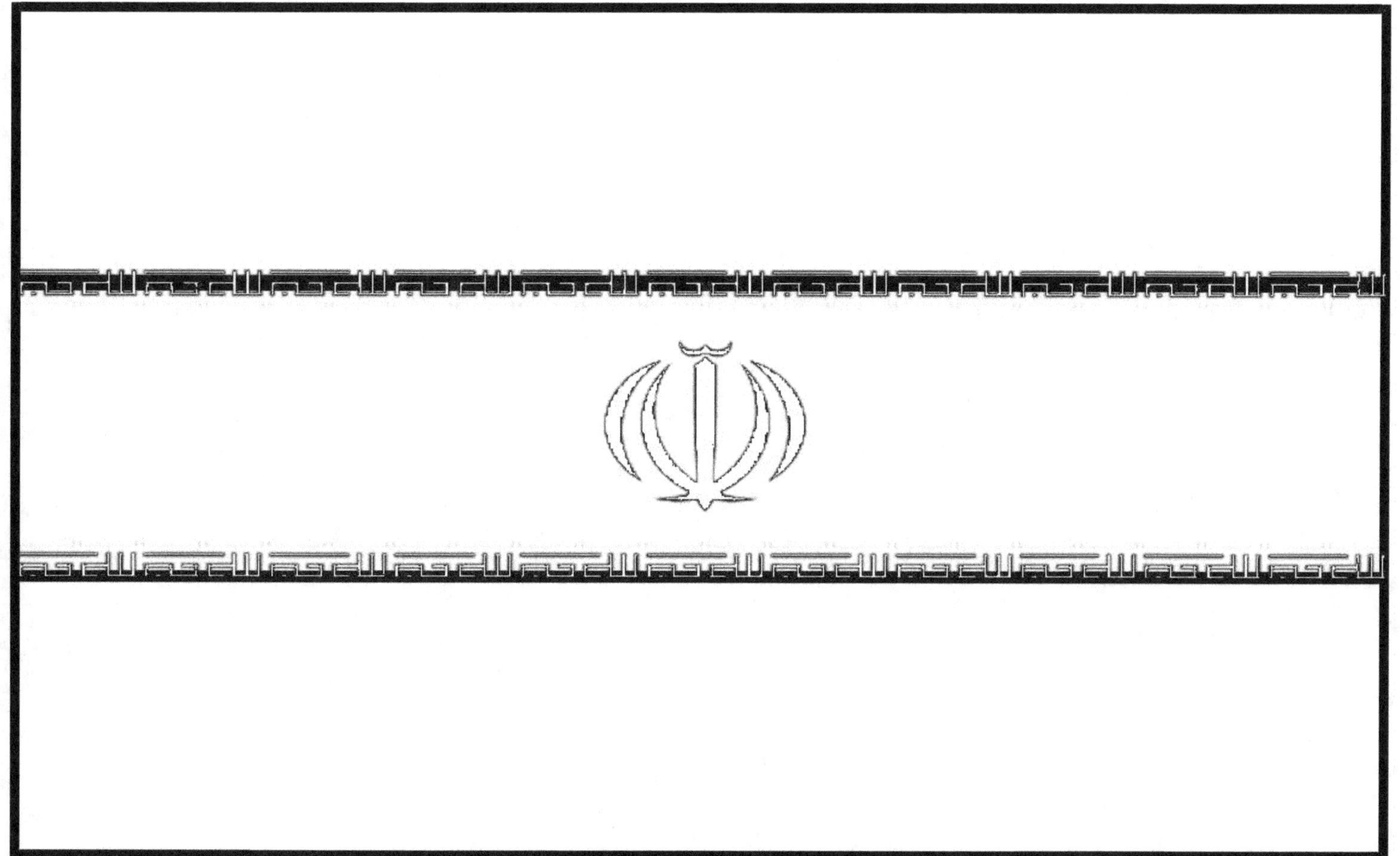

Iran

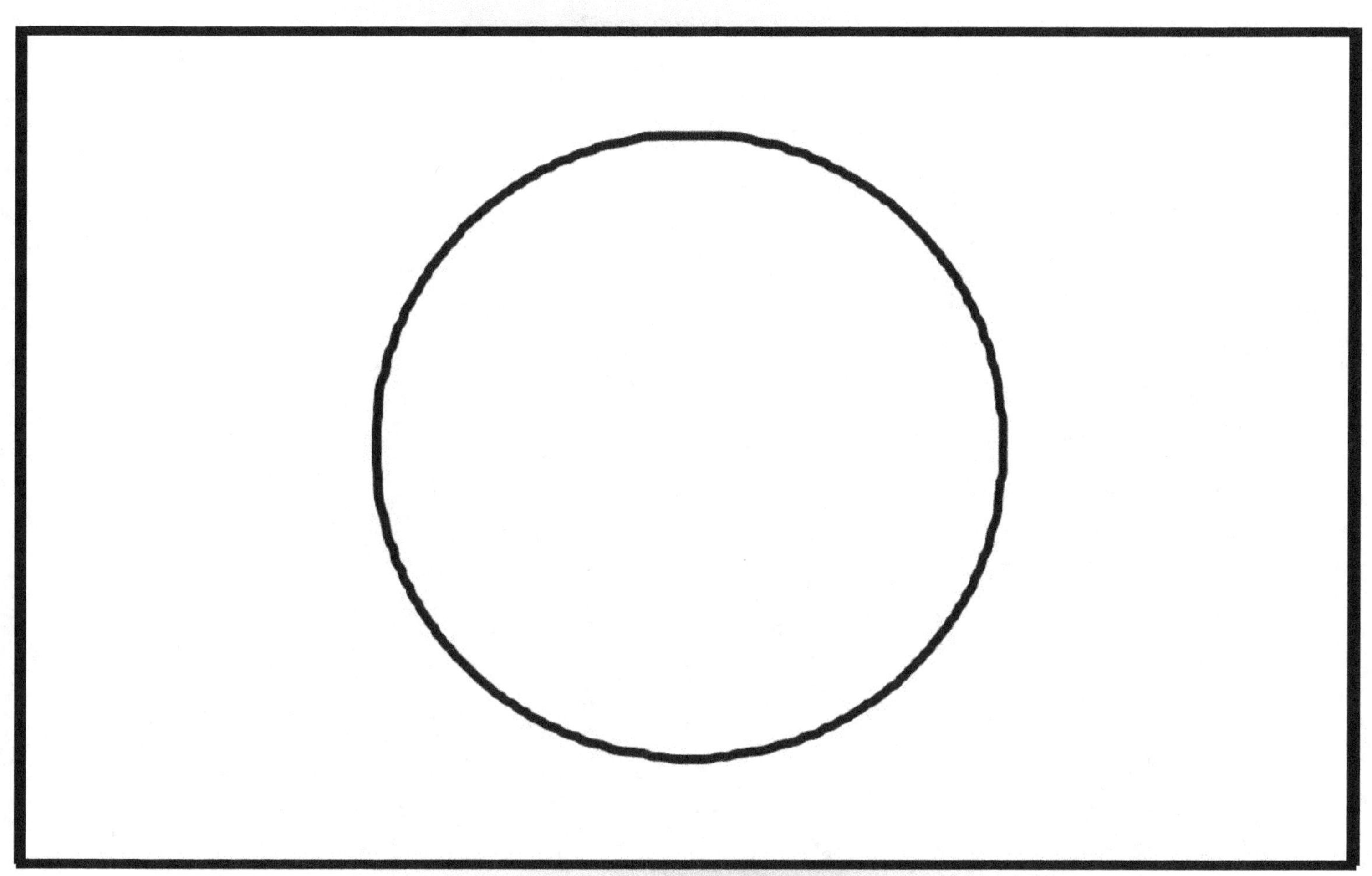

JAPAN

NEW ZELAND

TURKEY

Find Out The Color Of This Flag

UNITED KINGDOM

MOROCCO

Find Out The Color Of This Flag

CHINA

Find Out The Color Of This Flag

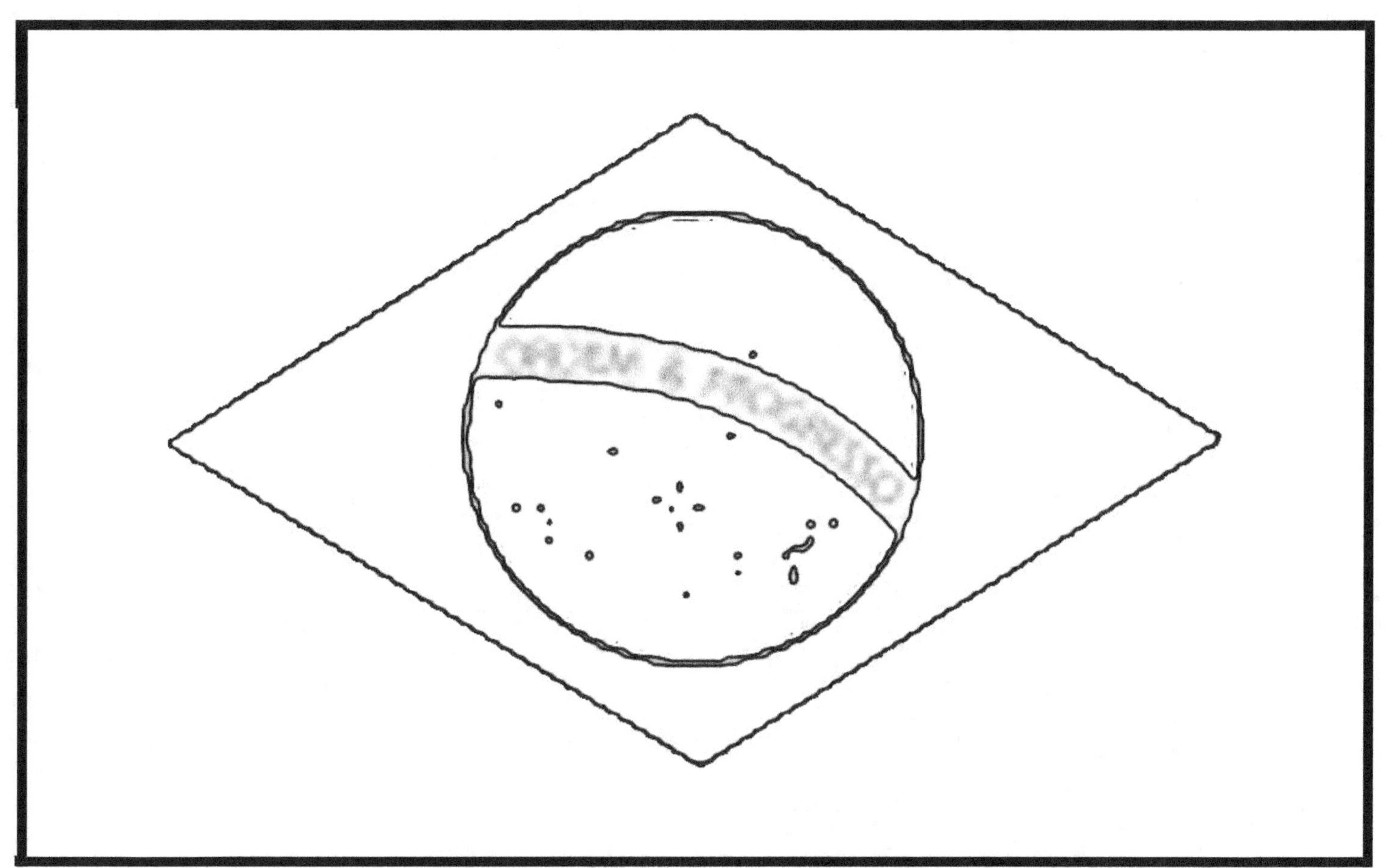

BRAZIL

CANADA

HANGARY

Find Out The Color Of This Flag

UNITED STATES

Find Out The Color Of This Flag

ITALY

FRANCE

MALI

NIGERIA

Find Out The Color Of This Flag

ROMANIA

IRLAND

Find Out The Color Of This Flag

CHAD

BELGIUM

SPAIN

Find Out The Color Of This Flag
AUSTRIA

Find Out The Color Of This Flag

SWEDEN

Find Out The Color Of This Flag

FINLAND

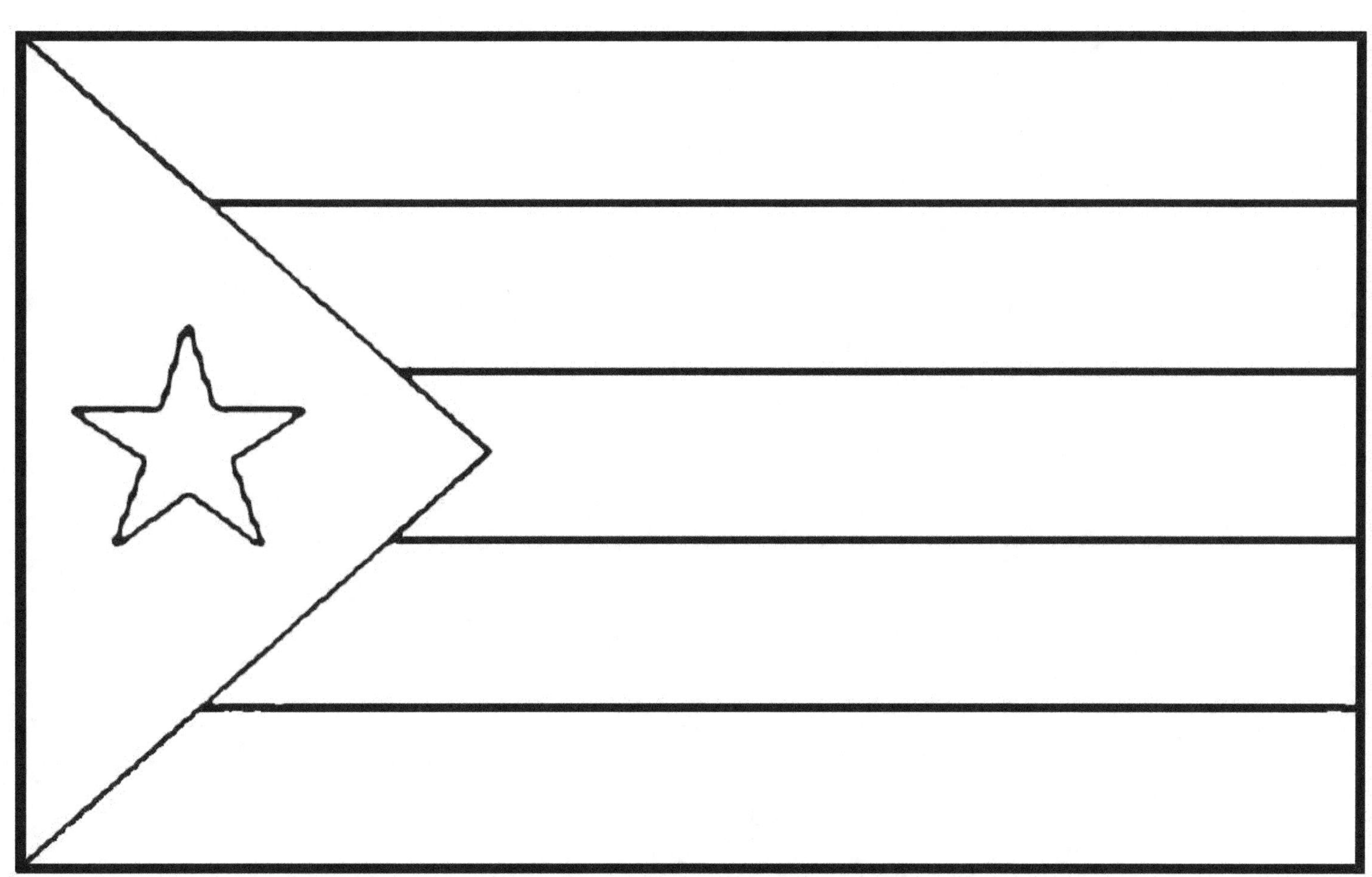

CUBA

COLOMBIA

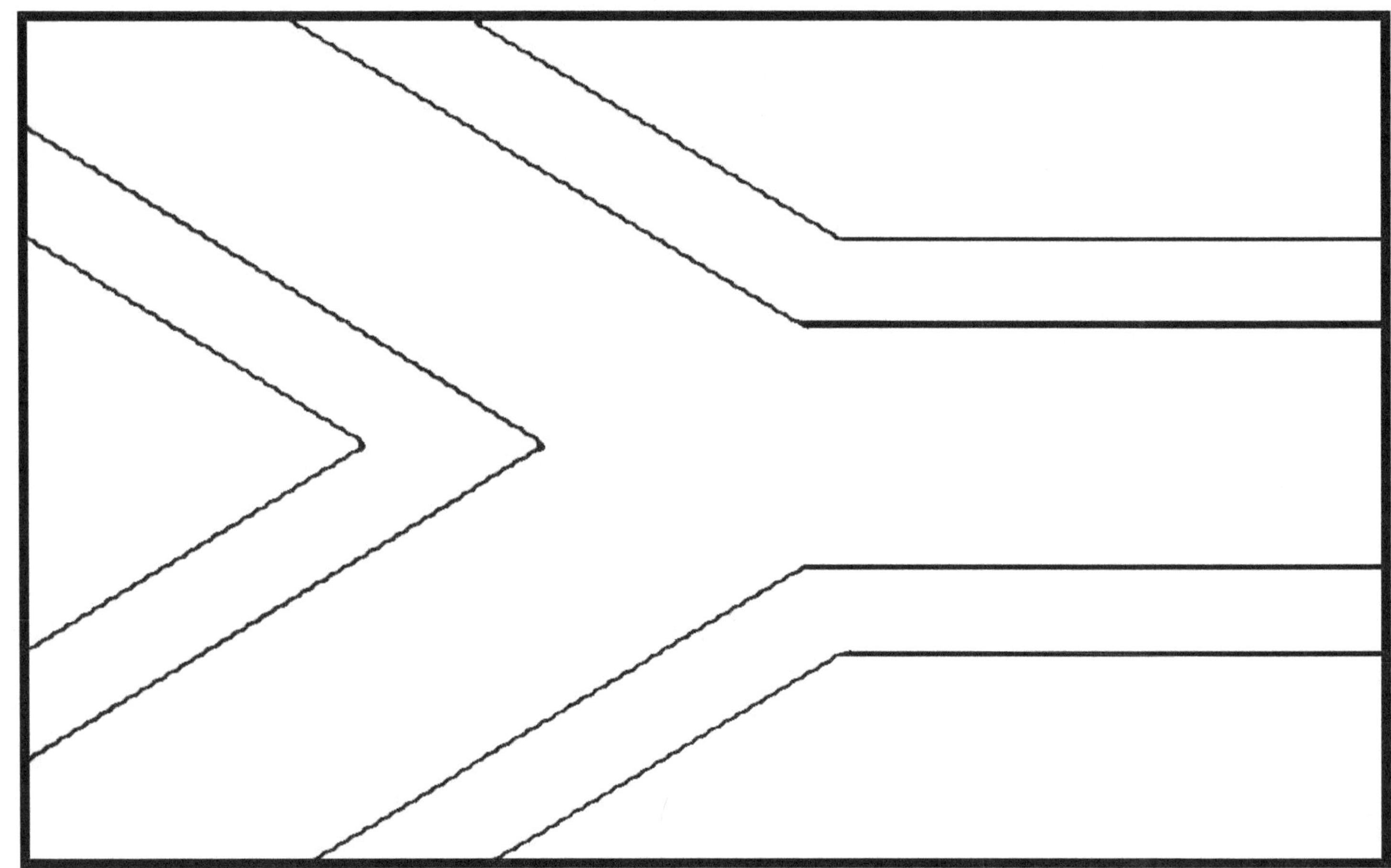

SOUTH AFRICA

GRECE

BULGARIA

ESTONIA

LITHUNIA

LUXEMBOURG